KARRI KOKKO

DREAMS BEFORE SLEEP

LYHYTTAVARA

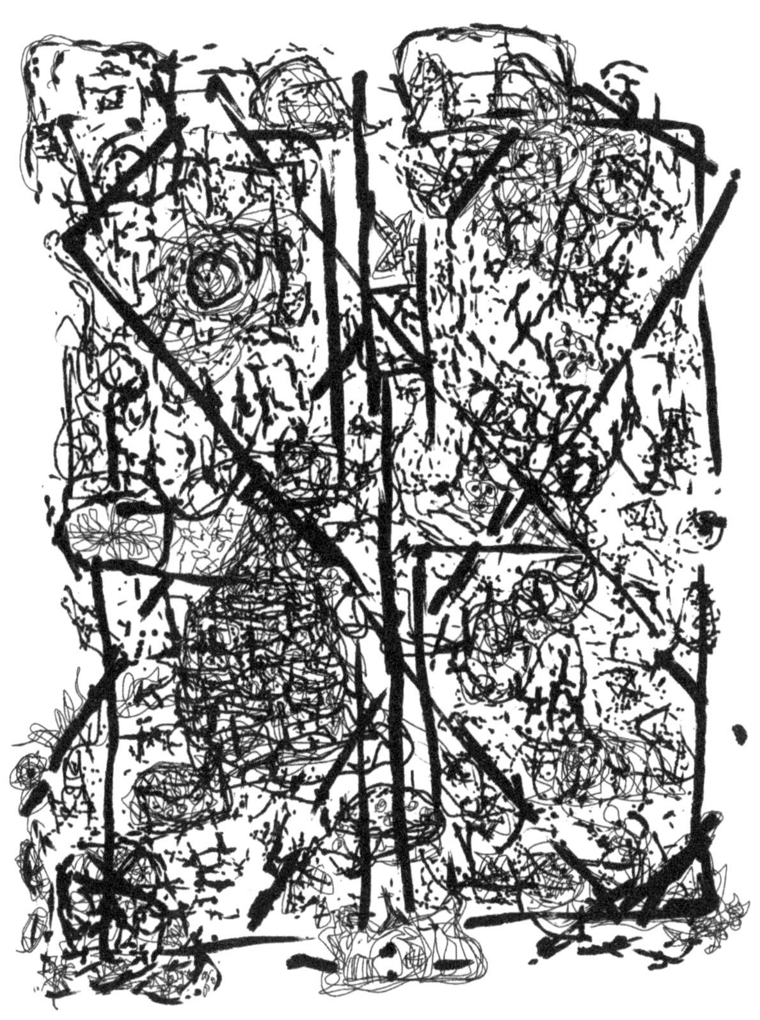

Picasso

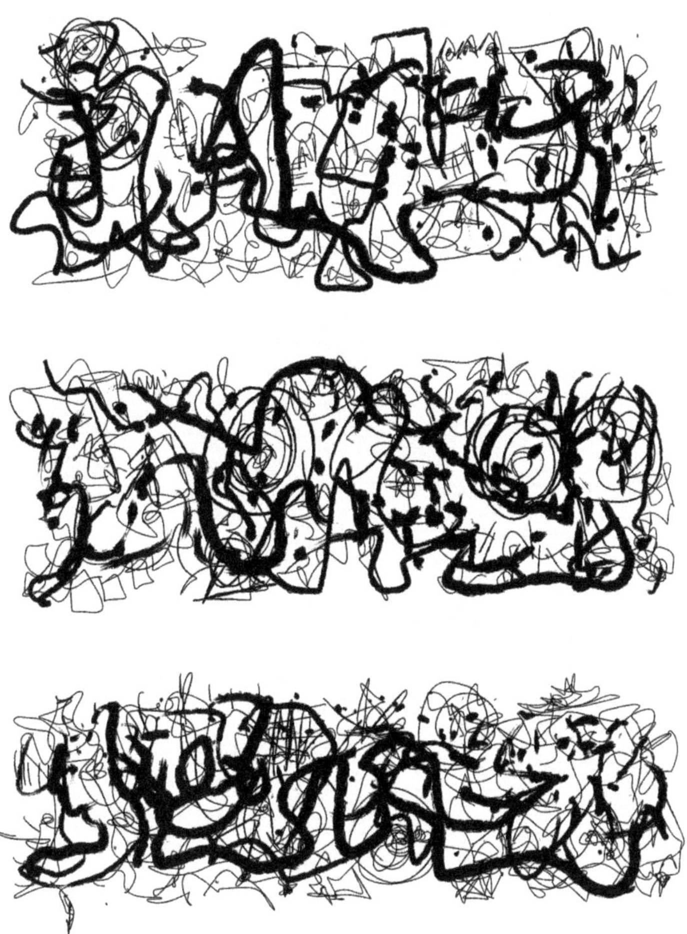

Making windows where there were once walls.

Lyhyttavara 2023

Graphic design and layout: Karri Kokko

ISBN: 978-952-65085-4-2

Printer: BoD – Books on Demand, Norderstedt, Germany

lyhyttavara@gmail.com

@ facebook | instagram | tumblr